THE LIVING FESTIVALS SERIES

Jack Priestley – Series Editor

Ascensiontide and Pentecost

FAY SAMPSON

RMEP

RELIGIOUS AND MORAL EDUCATION PRESS

A Member of the Pergamon Group of Companies

Religious and Moral Education Press
A Member of the Pergamon Group of Companies
Hennock Road, Exeter EX2 8RP

Pergamon Press Ltd
Headington Hill Hall, Oxford OX3 0BW

Pergamon Press Inc.
Maxwell House, Fairview Park, Elmsford, New York 10523

Pergamon Press Canada Ltd
Suite 104, 150 Consumers Road, Willowdale, Ontario M2J 1P9

Pergamon Press (Australia) Pty Ltd
P.O. Box 544, Potts Point, N.S.W. 2011

Pergamon Press GmbH
Hammerweg 6, D-6242 Kronberg, Federal Republic of Germany

First published 1986

Printed in Great Britain by A. Wheaton & Co. Ltd, Hennock Road, Exeter

ISBN 0 08-031774-X non net
      0 08-031775-8 net

ACKNOWLEDGEMENTS
The author and publisher wish to thank the following organizations and individuals who kindly provided photographs:

Baptist Times
BBC Hulton Picture Library
Britain/Israel Public Affairs
  Committee
Burnley Express & News
Keith Ellis
Gloucestershire Newspapers Ltd

The Mansell Collection
Northamptonshire Evening Telegraph
Brian Shuel
United Society for the Propagation
  of the Gospel
J. Wippell & Co. Ltd, Exeter

The cover photograph, by Brian Shuel, shows a well-dressing at Tideswell, Derbyshire.

Contents

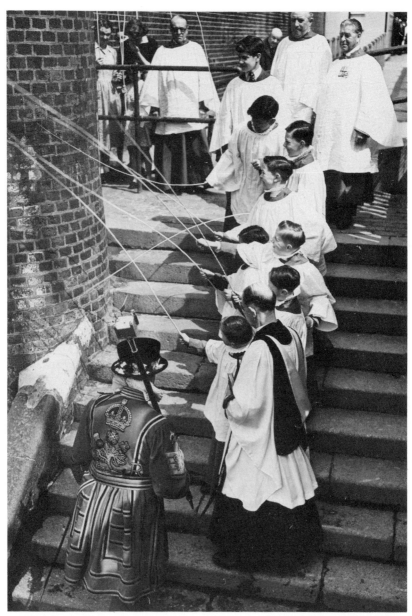

Beating the bounds at the Tower of London: one of the interesting local customs associated with Ascension Day.

Introduction

The Christian year begins with Advent, when we prepare for the coming of Jesus and the first great festival of Christmas. It reaches its highest point in spring, with the festival of Christ's Resurrection, Easter Sunday. Forty days later comes Ascension Day, when Christ was seen by his followers for the last time and returned to his Father. You might think that this would be the end of the story. But it is not. There is a third great Christian festival still to come. Do you know what it is?

Seven weeks after Easter comes Pentecost, or Whit Sunday. To Christians this is not an ending, but a great beginning. It celebrates the coming of the Holy Spirit. It is the birthday of the Christian Church. (In the Jewish calendar, Pentecost is a harvest festival, the Feast of Weeks.)

This festival is about water and wind and flames. If you go into a church at Pentecost, the colours you will see are white and red. White is the colour of purity. New Christians used to wear white robes for baptism at Pentecost, and so it became called 'White Sunday'. Red is the colour of life. It is a symbol of the Holy Spirit, the life-giver.

The Ascension. Stained-glass window in the church at Temple, Cornwall.

1

The Bible Story

The Christian festivals of Ascension and Pentecost (Whitsun) come from Bible stories which tell of the events following the Resurrection of Jesus. They explain how a small group of frightened men and women became the forerunners of a worldwide Church.

The Ascension (Matt. 28: 16–20; Mark 16: 19–20; Luke 24: 44–52; Acts 1: 6–11)
When Jesus was crucified, the men and women who had followed him were plunged into grief and fear. For three years they had travelled the country with him as he taught about God the Father and healed the sick. They thought the Kingdom of God had come on earth. Now they had lost their Master. They could not understand what had gone wrong.

Then, two days later, Mary Magdalene came running to tell them that Jesus had risen from the dead and had appeared to her. At first they did not believe her. But Jesus showed himself to two others and then to all of them. They knew joyfully that it was really true.

Jesus came to them many times. His Resurrection body was strange, but it was still the same Jesus they had known. Each time he appeared, he talked to them about what they must do next. But they expected they would always go on seeing him as before. They waited eagerly for the next time he would come to them.

Then one day Jesus led them to the top of a hill overlooking Jerusalem. He repeated a promise he had made to them before his crucifixion. He said that the Holy Spirit would come to them. He told them they must now go out into the whole world and spread the good news about everything he had done.

When he had finished speaking, a cloud came down and settled over the hilltop where Jesus was standing. As it lifted into the sky, they saw that he was no longer with them. As they stood open-mouthed, gazing up after the cloud, they saw two men in white, who had not been there before, smiling at them.

'You people from Galilee, why are you standing looking up into heaven? This same Jesus that you have seen ascend into heaven, shall come again in the same way that you have seen him go' (Acts 1:11).

Then they understood what Jesus had done. His work on earth was finished. He had handed over the task to them to carry on.

Pentecost (Acts 2)

Jesus's followers went back to Jerusalem and began to make plans for the future. There were the eleven Apostles (Judas Iscariot, who betrayed Jesus, was now dead), Jesus's mother and other members of his family, and many women and men who called themselves his friends.

They chose Matthias to take the place of Judas. They met daily to pray together. They shared bread and wine, remembering the Last Supper and the Crucifixion.

Amongst themselves they shared the joy and wonder of the Resurrection. But they had not dared to tell anyone else. Jerusalem was still a dangerous place for them. Jesus had many powerful enemies: the council of priests in the Temple; King Herod; the governor, Pilate, who wanted to keep the peace of the Roman Empire at any price.

Jesus had been crucified at the feast of Passover, in the spring. Now it was seven weeks later, and there was another festival in Jerusalem, the Jewish feast of Pentecost. The city was packed with strangers. Roman soldiers patrolled the streets, watching for trouble-makers.

On that morning in Jerusalem, the followers of Jesus met as usual in an upstairs room. As they prayed together, something tremendous happened to them. It seemed as though a strong wind rushed through the house. At the same time they felt as though they were being set on fire. They looked round in astonishment. Later, when they described what happened they said they saw flames on everyone else's head.

Suddenly they realized what Jesus had meant when he said

The Coming of the Holy Spirit (ascribed to Andrea da Firenze).

they must tell the whole world about what he had done. Without thinking about their own safety, they ran out of the house. The streets were crowded with pilgrims. Then all the followers of Jesus seemed to be talking at once. Some of those who heard them said they must be drunk. But now waves of amazement were running through the crowd. They realized that all the foreigners there, from Europe, from Africa, from Asia, no matter what language they spoke, could understand the words that were being said.

Peter took the lead. He jumped up on to a platform and began to shout to the people. He told them how the prophets had foretold the coming of the Son of God, who had now come to them as Jesus of Nazareth. He told them how Jesus had been crucified, only to rise again to bring life and forgiveness to everyone who followed him. He called upon every man and woman present to turn to Jesus. Hundreds of them asked to be baptized. From that day of Pentecost, the Christian Church spread rapidly.

Peter and John were soon arrested and put in prison. But it was too late to stop what had begun. The message was already going out across the world.

The men and women who had felt this power, like rushing wind and flames, said they had been filled with the Holy Spirit.

The spread of the Church

The first Christians were Jews. But soon it seemed as if the Holy Spirit was moving ahead of the disciples. Acts 10 describes how a Roman centurion in the port of Joppa sent a message to Peter asking him to come to his house and speak to the people there too. Peter was a strict Jew who did not mix with non-Jews (Gentiles). But a vision from God told him to follow the messenger. While he was still speaking about Jesus Christ to the people in the centurion's house, the hearers were filled with the Holy Spirit. Peter and the Jews with him were astonished. They realized that Christianity was for the Gentiles too, and they baptized all who were there.

Travellers like St Paul and St Thomas went to many countries preaching the good news of Jesus. But as the Church grew, so its enemies became determined to stamp it out. The Roman Emperors were afraid because Christians would no longer salute them as gods. Faced with the choice, many Christians died as martyrs rather than deny their loyalty to Christ the King. In spite of the persecutions, the Church continued to spread till, in the fourth century, the Emperor Constantine himself became a Christian.

Pentecost tells of the coming of a power that gave people the courage to speak out in front of others, to travel the world spreading their faith, and if necessary to die for it. This power of the Holy Spirit is still celebrated at Whitsun.

2

Pentecost Today

Ascension Day and Pentecost, ten days later, are high points in the Christian year. Shavuoth, the Jewish feast of Pentecost, has grown in meaning since biblical times. Throughout the Christian year, the belief in the power of the Holy Spirit is alive in the rites of baptism and confirmation, in the worship of Pentecostals and in the lives and witness of Christians all over the world.

Ascension Day

Ascension Day is the sixth Thursday after Easter. It marks the day when Jesus appeared to his friends for the last time. In some churches, the Paschal candle that has burned since Easter is put out. You might think that this would be a sad occasion. But it is not. Christians believe that at the Ascension, Christ returned to his heavenly Father in triumph. He had defeated death and sin. He had opened heaven to everyone who followed him. It is a time for rejoicing.

Ascensiontide is a traditional time for open-air processions. In the Middle Ages people acted out the journey of Jesus and his disciples to the Mount of Olives. In Chapter 3 you will read about some walks of witness that are still held.

Another custom is to lift up a statue of Jesus during a service. In some churches it was hoisted through a hole in the roof!

Some Church schools attend a service on Ascension Day and then take the rest of the day as a holiday. 'Holiday' means 'holy day'.

Shavuoth

The Jewish festival of Pentecost comes fifty days after Passover. 'Pentecost' is a Greek word meaning 'fiftieth'. The Hebrew name 'Shavuoth' means 'Feast of Weeks', because there are seven times seven days – a week of weeks – between Passover and Pentecost. Other names are 'Feast of Harvest' and 'Day of First Fruits'.

Shavuoth began as a harvest festival. In Israel (where the growing season is early) it falls at the beginning of the wheat harvest. When the Temple was standing in Jerusalem, people offered the first fruits of their harvest there, as a sign of their gratitude to God.

Today synagogues are still decorated with corn. The story of Ruth is read. Ruth was a foreigner and a widow who came to Judaea. Because she had no money, she was allowed to gather

Children celebrating Shavuoth at the Western Wall, Jerusalem.

13

the corn the reapers had dropped. But there is more to the story of Ruth than that. It tells of the faithfulness of a Gentile who followed the God of the Jews.

In the same way, Shavuoth has grown into something much more than a harvest festival. On that day one of the greatest stories in the history of Israel is read. It tells how God gave His Law to Moses on Mount Sinai, while the Israelites were on their long journey from Egypt to the Promised Land. An agreement, or Covenant, was made between God and the people of Israel. Each promised to be faithful to the other (Exodus 20–23). Shavuoth is now the day of celebration of the gift of God's Law, the Torah.

In the twentieth century it has become a day of confirmation for Jewish boys and girls, who declare their resolve to follow God's Law at a special synagogue service.

Christian Pentecost

Christians saw new meanings for both the Covenant and harvest. They honoured Moses, who had given them God's Law. But they saw Jesus Christ as the bringer of a New Covenant, which offered them forgiveness for sin and promised eternal life. They believed that the gift of the Holy Spirit symbolized the 'first fruits' of this New Covenant.

Pentecost became the time when new believers entered the Covenant by joining the Church. Since earliest times it has been one of the three great festivals of the Christian year. Special services of Holy Communion are held. Churches are decorated with altar-hangings of red, and flower-arrangements of red, or red and white. Priests wear red vestments. Red is the symbol of the Holy Spirit.

Baptism

Water is one of the great symbols of Whitsuntide. Water gives life. Baptism is a sign of a new beginning in the Christian life.

From early times, the birthday of the Christian Church seemed a good choice for people to make their first promises to Christ. New believers were baptized, often by walking into

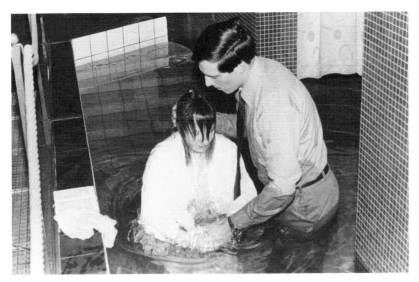
Baptist baptism ceremony.

water and being dipped right under (total immersion), as a sign of washing away their sins and rising to a new life with Christ. Sometimes they received the gift of the Holy Spirit at their baptism. In other cases one of the leading disciples would come later and lay hands on the baptized person, who would burst out into a strange language. This is known as 'speaking in tongues'. Later, it became the custom for those who were being baptized to wear white robes. They kept them on for seven days to show the world that they had been washed clean from sin. That is how Pentecost became known as 'White' or 'Whit' Sunday.

It is still traditional for babies to wear white robes for baptism. Some Churches, like the Baptists, do not think it right to baptize babies. They wait until people are old enough to decide for themselves, usually as teenagers or adults. Many Churches, including the Baptists, still use the symbol of baptism by total immersion. The new Christians at this ceremony usually wear a white gown or a white shirt. The name given to ceremonies where teenage or older people are baptized is 'believers' baptism'.

Confirmation

Nowadays many Churches baptize the babies of Christian parents some weeks after they are born. But in the Western Churches it is felt these children need to renew the promises made for them at baptism. It is important to do this when they are old enough to understand the promises for themselves.

The service at which this is done is often called 'confirmation'. The bishop, or in some Churches the minister, lays hands on the head of the believer. It is a symbol that they have received the gift of the Holy Spirit. In the Roman Catholic Church they are anointed with oil and struck on the cheek as a sign of the spiritual warfare they have entered. In the Eastern Orthodox Church confirmation follows immediately after baptism, even for infants.

White is the traditional colour for confirmation dresses.

Anglican bishop with confirmation candidates.

16

Speaking in tongues

The story of Pentecost, with the Apostles speaking to crowds from many countries, makes it sound as if the 'gift of tongues' was the ability to speak in foreign languages. Later stories in the Acts of the Apostles and the Letters of Paul show that the early believers would sometimes break out into a speech like no human language known anywhere in the world. It needed someone else who had received the power of the Spirit to interpret the meaning of the words. At first it was expected as a true sign of baptism by the Holy Spirit. But in his letter to the Corinthians, Paul warns that speaking in tongues is important but not as useful as prophesying (speaking out) the will of God in plain language.

Speaking in tongues *(glossolalia)* can still be heard in many Churches which have a strong belief in the power of the Holy Spirit.

Pentecostal Churches

'Pentecostals' are Christians who believe that the 'baptism of the Spirit' still falls upon people as it did in New Testament times. They expect to have the experience of speaking in tongues. This baptism of the Spirit is a second stage, following their earlier conversion to Christ.

There are Pentecostal Churches throughout the world. In Britain, the best known are the Elim Pentecostal Church and the Assemblies of God. There are also a great number of smaller Pentecostal Churches brought over by West Indian immigrants. In their worship they try to be as open as possible to the Spirit. One person may break out into an unknown language and, whenever possible, someone else will interpret the words. At other times people will find themselves singing or praying in tongues. It is not necessary always to know the meaning; it is the feeling of worship which counts.

Pentecostal Christians believe in worshipping with their bodies too. During hymns or prayers some wave their hands in the air, or begin to shake uncontrollably. They may dance in the aisles, or even roll on the ground. They believe it is

Pentecostal Christians, Buenos Aires.

right for worship to involve the emotions as well as the mind.

Besides the Pentecostal Churches which have sprung up in the twentieth century, there are Pentecostal Christians in the older denominations, from Roman Catholics to Quakers. For most of them, speaking in tongues is likely to happen not in front of the congregation at Sunday worship, but in private prayer, or perhaps in a small prayer-group of fellow Pentecostals.

In recent years there has been a growth of 'charismatic' Christians in all denominations of the Church. 'Charisma' means 'gift'. Like the Pentecostals, charismatic Christians expect the gifts of the Spirit. They are ready to be moved and guided in unexpected and joyful ways. But they believe that speaking in tongues is only one amongst many gifts, and not necessary for everyone.

3

Celebrations

Long before Christianity came to Europe, there were great summer festivals. May Day and Midsummer were the most important of these. But as Christianity took over from the older religions, some celebrations moved to the feast days of the Christian calendar, while others kept to the traditional date. So all over Europe, you can see similar ceremonies performed on May Day, Ascension Day, Whit Sunday or Monday, and Midsummer's Eve or Midsummer Day, or indeed any weekend in summer!

If you want to check what is on near you, be careful about the dates. Whit Monday used to be a public holiday. Now we have the Spring Bank Holiday instead. Some traditional Whitsun customs have now moved to this day. It is made more confusing when people wrongly call this new holiday 'Whit-sun'. It is only occasionally that they fall on the same weekend.

Ascension Day is always on a Thursday, forty days after Easter. The Church still celebrates Pentecost, or Whit Sunday, seven weeks after Easter, in late May or early June.

Some folk customs have been transformed into Christian ceremonies. Old gods and goddesses have been replaced in many customs by Jesus Christ and the Virgin Mary. The life-giving symbols of water and sun now stand for God the Holy Spirit and the Son of God. Others customs have remained clearly pagan.

Rogationtide

The Sunday before Ascension Day is Rogation Sunday, and the Monday, Tuesday and Wednesday of that week are Rogation Days. In Latin, 'rogatio' means 'asking', or 'entreaty'. In northern Europe Rogationtide is a time for asking God's blessing on the growing crops. Processions are held around the parish, led by the priest and the cross. Prayers are said over the fields. In seaside parishes the priest may go out on the jetty and bless the sea and the fishing boats.

Beating the bounds

The Romans held a festival called Terminalia, sacred to Terminus, the god of boundaries. In Christian times, Rogationtide and Ascension Day processions became a way of fixing the boundaries of the parish in everyone's memory, particularly the young boys'.

It was the custom to 'beat the bounds'. At every landmark, such as a stone or a tree or a stream, a boy would be beaten with willow wands, or held upside down and bumped, or ducked in the water. Many parishes still keep up the custom, or have revived it recently.

Choirboys in procession at the Tower of London, ready to beat the bounds.

20

One colourful example of such a ceremony is at the Tower of London. On Ascension Day, every three years, a grand procession makes its way around the area of land called the Tower Liberty, pausing at the Crown Boundary Marks. It is led by the Chief Yeoman Warder, in his Tudor uniform of red and gold, and the Tower Chaplain. Behind come a local church choir, the children of the Tower, and the Governor and his staff, with their families, with the Yeoman Warders marching on either side. The Yeoman Gaoler brings up the rear.

At each mark the Chaplain calls, 'Cursed is he that removeth his neighbour's land mark.' The Chief Warder orders, 'Whack it, boys!' In this case it is the children who beat the mark with their willow wands. The ceremony is made even more lively when it clashes with the rival procession from the next-door parish of All Hallows.

It seems that the ceremony is still necessary. The procession in 1984 found that the Gas Board had accidentally removed one of the boundary stones.

Whit Walks
When the Nonconformist Churches broke away from the Church of England, they tended to drop the traditional ceremonies of the Christian year, believing them to be superstitions. But in the industrial North and Wales, where Nonconformity was strongest, they play an important part in processions of witness in the early summer, often at Whitsuntide. These parades are known as 'Whit Walks' or 'Walking Days'.

The largest Whit Walks are in the city of Manchester, where Roman Catholics, Anglicans and Nonconformist Churches all hold their own processions. In 1899 there were 25000 children in one parade. Today thousands still take part.

The more colourful parades have religious tableaux on lorries. At the head of the procession is a band. There are Sunday-school banners, and it is a great honour for a child to carry a banner pole or to hold one of the tasselled ropes that hang from it. Behind the children come grown-up members of

Whit Walk at Padiham, Lancashire. Sunday-school children and their queen.

the church. The walk often ends with a picnic in a field or a church hall.

It was traditional in many churches for the girls to wear white, and the shops would be full of white dresses for weeks beforehand.

Well-dressing

The theme of water recurs in Whitsuntide customs. Before the days of reservoirs and pumping stations, people depended on natural springs and wells. The great fear of summer was drought. Wells and springs have been thought of as sacred for thousands of years. They were often believed to be the home of a water-spirit or goddess, and offerings were made to her. Later this became a Christian thanksgiving to God for the gift of water.

In Derbyshire the custom of well-dressing is still a great art, often passed on from father to son. First a board is covered with smooth clay. A picture, with a religious subject, is drawn on it. Then the whole design is filled in with a beautiful assortment of flowers, berries, moss, shells, or any other natural objects, but never anything manufactured, like metal or glass. Lastly the picture is carefully put in position behind or above the well.

One of the most famous well-dressing ceremonies takes place at Tissington on Ascension Day. There are five wells in Tissington, which are said to have supplied water even in the longest drought. The ceremony starts with a service of

Well-dressing and collecting-box for charity in Hope, Derbyshire.

23

thanksgiving in the church and then the procession makes its way around all the wells, which have already been decorated by the well-dressers. A tradition says that this ceremony is a thank-offering because Tissington escaped the plague called the Black Death in 1350. It may have been revived then, but the custom is likely to be much older.

At Wirksworth there is a Queen of the Wells. But the well-dressings are placed at the site of the now-vanished public taps! They are a thank-offering for the piped water which reached the village in 1840. Here the ceremonies take place on the Saturday of the Spring Bank Holiday weekend.

Church Ale

A poem of 1671 says:

> The churches much owe, as we all do knowe
> For when they be drooping and ready to fail
> By a Whitsun or Church-Ale up again they shall go,
> And owe their repairing to a pot of good ale.
> Ex-ale-tation of Ale. Peter Mews

The Church Ale was a way of raising money for church funds from very early times. The churchwardens begged or bought malt, and the ale was brewed in the Church House, which served as the parish hall. Everyone in the parish was expected to come along and to pay a few pence for their ale. Church Ales were times when young and old, high and low, came together for merrymaking and enjoyment. They could be held at any time of year, but Whitsun was a popular choice for summer celebrations.

This idea of a parish feast in which everyone can join has been revived in modern times. There are many Christian Churches. They often find it difficult to share a service of Holy Communion, because of their different beliefs about it. But in some parishes Pentecost has become the time for churches to join together in sharing a supper or picnic. The idea of a shared meal, the 'Agape' or love-feast, goes back to New Testament times.

24

Ram-roasting

Some village ram-roasts have histories that go back to the days of pre-Christian sacrifice.

One such ceremony is the Ram Fair held at Kingsteignton in Devon on Whit Monday. Today the carcase of a lamb is decorated and carried through the streets. It is roasted on a spit while sports and maypole dancing go on around it. In past times a live lamb used to be decked with flowers and ribbons and carried through the streets on a flower-hung cart on Whit Monday. On the Tuesday it was killed and the decorated carcase was wheeled on a handbarrow to the roasting.

Tradition says that in earlier times, the stream that flows through the churchyard was stopped for this ceremony, and the ram was roasted on the bed of the leat. This was said to be a celebration of the time when, in pre-Christian days, the stream failed but flowed again after a ram was sacrificed here.

In Oxfordshire, Trinity Monday, a week after Whit Monday, was the traditional time for the Lamb Ale. At Kidlington, girls used to chase the sacrificial lamb. They had their thumbs tied behind their backs and the one who caught it with her mouth was declared the Lady of the Lamb. In the parish of Kirtlington there is still a Lamb Ale on Trinity Monday. There is a church service, sports, Morris dancing, and a dinner at which the main dish is roast lamb. But there is no longer a Lord and Lady, nor the traditional procession with a live lamb carried on a man's shoulders.

Cheese rolling

One of the customs which has moved from Whit Monday to the Spring Bank Holiday is the rolling of a cheese down Cooper's Hill in the parish of Brockworth in Gloucestershire. At the top of the hill stands a maypole decorated with flowers. The race is supervised by a Master of Ceremonies who wears a white coat and a top hat decked with ribbons. He hands the whole cheese, protected by a wooden case, to the Starter and begins to count. At the count of three, the Starter sends the cheese bouncing down the steep hill. At four, the competitors

Chasing a cheese down Cooper's Hill.

go racing after it. The winner, the first to reach the cheese at the bottom of the hill, keeps it. There are several races, for young men, for girls, and so on.

Some say there is a connection between the yellow cheese rolling round and round and the movement of the sun. In pre-Christian times this was a magic ceremony to give power to the sun as it neared the longest day and had to battle against the growing darkness again.

Another Whit Monday race used to start from the White Horse at Uffington, a great figure carved out of the chalk hillside in the Iron Age. Every few years the Horse was ceremonially cleaned or 'scoured'. Then young men raced down the gully below the head, called the Manger, chasing a cartwheel. Again, the prize was a cheese.

Rush strewing

Another pleasant custom is the strewing of freshly-cut rushes in churches during the summer. At the Church of St Mary Redcliffe in Bristol, this is still done on Whit Sunday. The Mayor comes to the church, where he is welcomed by the Bishop of Bristol to a fanfare of trumpets. The floor of the church is strewn with rushes and there is a posy of flowers for each member of the congregation.

Rushes strewn in the aisle of St Mary Redcliffe.

This is a remnant of the days when churches were cold and damp. Their stone or earth floors used to be covered with a carpet of rushes, and each summer these would be renewed. In some parishes, the fresh rushes were brought to church on a decorated wagon. In others they were carried by young women dressed in white with garlands of flowers, accompanied by Morris dancers.

Rush Sunday posies.

Dicing for Bibles

St Ives in Cambridgeshire has its own curious Whitsun custom. In a will dated 1675, Dr Robert Wilde left money for Bibles to be won by poor children in a game of dice. Today twelve children are chosen to dice for six Bibles. Six of the children are from the Church of England and six from Nonconformist Churches.

At first the dice were thrown on the altar itself. Later it was thought that this was not a fit place, and the game was moved to a table near the chancel steps, and then to the church school. Now it has returned to the table inside the church.

The Dunmow Flitch

Once every four years, married couples in Essex also have a chance to win a prize if they are brave enough to stand before a mock court and have their married life examined in detail. A husband and wife must claim that for a year and a day they have never once quarrelled or regretted their marriage. The trial usually takes place in the village of Great Dunmow on Whit Monday, though occasionally it is held elsewhere.

There is a judge, counsel for both sides, and a jury of six

Children giving evidence at their parents' Dunmow Flitch trial, 1926.

bachelors and six spinsters. The court will ask for evidence that the couple are telling the truth, or invite witnesses to prove the claim untrue. It is usually an occasion for much laughter and joking. The couple who are judged to be telling the truth win a side of bacon, called a 'flitch'.

Formerly, the trial was held in the village of Little Dunmow. Only the husband could apply, and he was made to kneel upon two sharp stones at the Priory before the Prior, the monks and the people, while his case was examined. Then as now, the winner was carried triumphantly in a special chair.

Whitsun fairs

Whit Monday is a traditional time for summer fairs. But you will have to wait a long time to see Corby Pole Fair, because it is held only once every twenty years. The next time will be in 2002!

On this day, the approach roads to the old village of Corby, on the edge of Corby New Town, are barred to traffic. Anyone on foot may be stopped and asked to pay a toll. If they refuse, they are arrested and carried through the streets, men on a pole, women in a chair. They are given one last chance to pay before being put in the stocks. Some people actually seem to enjoy the experience!

This old custom may date back to the Danish Vikings,

Riding the stang.

who invaded this part of Britain. They had a form of punishment in which men were carried on a pole. It was called 'riding the stang'.

In 1585 Queen Elizabeth I granted a charter to the village of Corby, allowing its people to travel anywhere in England without paying tolls. A special Pole Fair was held in 1985 to celebrate the three-hundredth anniversary of the charter.

The cathedral city of Lichfield has its own Whitsun fair, now moved to the Spring Bank Holiday. It combines two traditions. One is the Greenhill Bower. Statues of saints, emblems of the

After the reading of the charter, the oldest man at the Fair, the rector of Corby and the council chairman are carried in procession through the streets.

trade guilds, and garlands of flowers used to be carried through the streets. Now there is a carnival procession. The other tradition is the Court of Array. All kinds of suits of armour and weapons are inspected by the Court in the Guildhall and paraded before the citizens at Greenhill.

All over Europe you will see customs like these. On Ascension Sunday the city of Venice is ceremonially 'married' to the sea when a golden ring is thrown into the waters of the Adriatic.

On the shores of the Atlantic, pilgrims come from all over Spain to the village of El Rocio at Whitsuntide. A statue of the Virgin and Child is decorated with fresh roses and carried in a great procession. But the names given to the statue in Spanish mean 'Our Lady of the Dew' and 'White Dove'. The feast of Whitsun with its symbols of water and the dove are more usually associated with the Holy Spirit and you can read more about their meaning in the next chapter.

4

The Meaning

In Britain, most people celebrate Christmas, whether they are Christians or not. At Easter, people enjoy chocolate eggs, even if they do not recognize they are a symbol of new life breaking out of the grave. But outside the Church, very few people notice the feasts of Ascension Day and Pentecost. The coming of the Holy Spirit is something that happens inside people. Even those to whom it happens find it difficult to put into words. You cannot see it happening. What you see is the change in people's lives.

Even the symbols that Christians use to describe the Holy Spirit are difficult to understand. Wind. Fire. Water. They are always moving. They seem to have a life of their own.

What do these symbols mean? What is the Holy Spirit? What did Jesus promise would happen at the first Pentecost?

The Spirit of Creation

At the very beginning of the Book of Genesis we read of a world covered with water. And the Spirit of God was 'brooding' over the surface of the waters. The word is that used for a mother-bird, who wants to give life.

The Hebrew word for 'spirit' is *ruach*. The writers of the Old Testament used the same word to mean 'wind'. It was the breath of life in humans and in God. The spirit of life sounded like a wind; the wind sweeping across the desert sand seemed like a living spirit. The Holy Spirit is the giver of life.

The Spirit in the gospels

The New Testament was written in Greek. The word for 'spirit' here is *pneuma*. Like the Hebrew *ruach*, it also means 'wind'.

In the early chapters of all four gospels, we find a picture strikingly like that at the start of the Old Testament. Again we are shown a new beginning. There is water and a brooding bird.

Jesus went down into the River Jordan to be baptized by his cousin John. As he rose from the water, both John the Baptist and Jesus saw the Spirit descend like a dove. John says he saw the Spirit settle over Jesus. A voice from heaven said, 'This is my beloved (or only) Son.'

The coming of the Son of God in the person of Jesus was like a second Creation. Again, the power of this new life came from

The Baptism of Christ, by Giovanni Bellini.

the Holy Spirit. The world was being given a chance to start again.

The same life-giving Holy Spirit overshadowed Mary before Jesus was born.

An old English name for the Holy Spirit was the 'Holy

34

Ghost'. We do not often use it now because 'ghost' has come to mean a spirit from the dead. The Holy Spirit, the giver of life, is the very opposite of that.

The Promise

In a beautiful passage from the Old Testament the prophet Joel heard God saying:

'I will pour out my spirit on all flesh; your sons and your daughters shall prophesy, your old men shall dream dreams, and your young men shall see visions. Even upon the menservants and maidservants in those days, I will pour out my spirit.'

(Joel 2:28–29)

Jesus promised his disciples that this would happen to them.

We read most about the gift of the Spirit in St John's account of the Last Supper (John 13–17). Jesus, knowing that he was about to die, said: 'I will pray the Father, and he will give you another Counsellor, to be with you for ever, even the Spirit of truth' (John 14:16).

The first English Bibles translated 'Counsellor' as 'Comforter'. But in those days that did not mean something soft and cuddly! A better word today would be 'Strengthener'. The Greek word *Paraclete*, from which the translation came, meant the sort of friend who would go to court with you and speak out for you in front of the judge and your accusers.

The very last time Jesus showed himself to the disciples after the Resurrection, he left them with this command:

'Wait for the promise of the Father, which you have heard from me, for John baptized with water, but before many days you shall be baptized with the Holy Spirit.

'You shall receive power when the Holy Spirit has come upon you; and you shall be my witnesses in Jerusalem and in all Judaea and Samaria and to the ends of the earth.'

(Acts 1:4–5, 8)

35

The meaning of the Ascension

Can you imagine yourself following Jesus for three years, hearing him preach to the crowds, watching him heal the sick, coming to believe he was the Son of God? Could you then imagine yourself taking over from him?

But Jesus knew that this is exactly what his disciples would have to do if his word was to be carried out across the whole world. The followers of Jesus would have to be changed into the leaders of his Church.

He had to hand on his task to them. And he needed to do it in a dramatic form, so that they would realize that he would not appear to them again until the end of time.

When the two men in white asked: 'Why are you standing looking up into heaven?' they were telling the disciples to come down to earth, to live in the present and work for the future.

Jesus had said that unless he went away from them, the Spirit would not come. Now the disciples were left alone. They knew that their own strength and wisdom were not enough for the task they had been given. They needed to realize how empty they were, before they could be filled with the inrushing power of the Holy Spirit.

The coming of the Holy Spirit

Ten days later they had an experience which they described as rushing wind and tongues of fire (Acts 2). It sent them running into the street, speaking in tongues and telling anyone who would listen about Jesus. They realized the gift Jesus had promised had come to them that day. They were the men and women the prophet Joel had described. They all said they were 'filled with the Holy Spirit'.

This is what Christians mean by the Holy Spirit. It is not something they believe *about* God. It is the action of God in their own life, guiding and strengthening them.

Modern Christians see the working of the Holy Spirit in many different ways. The older denominations of the Church hold a strong faith in the sacraments. They believe that at baptism and confirmation Christians receive the gift of the Holy Spirit in a very special way. They then have a power in their lives which they would not otherwise have. Pentecostals and other charismatic Christians expect the Spirit to take possession of them during worship, causing them to speak with tongues or to break out into praise or prayer. Quakers (the Society of Friends) begin their worship in silence. Nothing is planned in advance. They wait until someone feels inspired by the Spirit. Only then will they speak, say a prayer, or suggest the singing of a hymn. But all Christians believe that the Holy Spirit will guide and lead them at moments of great decision and in their everyday lives, if only they will be still and listen and follow.

The Trinity

The first Christians prayed to God as their 'Father'. They had known Jesus and his wonderful acts, and called him their 'Lord'. Now they felt filled with a power and wisdom and courage which they were sure came from the invisible presence of God. It was many years before they were able to explain what all this meant.

For over 1500 years, Christians have used the Nicene Creed to declare their belief in 'One God, the Father, the Almighty, maker of heaven and earth . . . one Lord, Jesus Christ, the only Son of God, begotten of the Father . . . and in the Holy Spirit, the Lord, the giver of life . . . who spoke by the prophets.'

Christians do not believe in three different gods. They are trying to express their feeling of knowing one God in three different ways: as Father and Ruler over all; as Son and Saviour, who by his life, death and resurrection reconciled human beings and God; and as Spirit and life-giver, the power that has inspired God's witnesses from Creation until now.

Once again, the symbol of water can help us. The Trinity is like the chemical compound H_2O which may be met as water, ice or steam, but which is not three different substances.

Trinity Sunday comes a week after Whit Sunday. It celebrates this Christian belief of three elements in one God.

Symbols of the Holy Spirit on church vestments worn at Pentecost.

Christians pray 'In the name of the Father, and of the Son, and of the Holy Spirit'. They believe that God the Son came to call people to do his Father's bidding on earth, and to show his love for his creation, even to the point of death. They believe that at the first Pentecost, it was God the Spirit who gave them the power to carry this message to all the world and to continue this work through the Christian Church.

THINGS TO DO

1 Make a picture in white and red to show the wind and fire of the Holy Spirit.

2 Arrange a visit to a local Anglican, Roman Catholic or Orthodox Christian church to see the vestments, altar-cloths and other hangings they use for Ascension Day or Pentecost.

3 There are many beautiful modern examples of church embroidery as well as traditional ones. Embroider a decoration for Ascension Day or Pentecost.

4 Look at a map of your area. Plan a Rogationtide procession. Which places would you stop to bless? Draw a map of your route, with pictures of the stopping-places.

5 Find out where the boundaries of your parish lie. Plan a walk around them and list the boundary marks you find.

6 No human words are great enough to describe God. We use many picture-words. Each one tells us something about God, but not everything. In Luke 15:3–6 Jesus compares God to a shepherd. In Luke 15:8–9 he describes God as a housewife. Read some of the other parables and see what picture we have of God in each story. In St John's gospel Jesus uses picture-words about himself. For example, 'I am the true vine' (John 15:1). See how many more you can find beginning 'I am'.

7 Make a well-dressing, using only natural materials. The picture-words for God may suggest a design.

8 The first two chapters of Genesis tell the story of Creation. Read them. Remember that in Hebrew *ruach* means both 'spirit' and 'breath'.

9 Make up a play in which a group of people learn that they will not see their leader again until some great task has been completed.

10 Choose a Christian denomination or another religion. Find out how people become members of this Church. Is there a service for babies? Is there a second ceremony, for older children or adults? What happens during these services?

MATERIAL FOR TEACHERS

Useful addresses

National Society for Promoting Religious Education
Church House
Dean's Yard
London SW1

Christian Education Movement
2 Chester House
Pages Lane
London N10 1PR

Books to read

Bull, Norman J. *Festivals and Customs.* Wheaton, 1979.
Elliott, Kathleen. *Festivals and Celebrations.* Young Library, 1984.
Green, Victor. *Festivals and Saints' Days.* Blandford, 1983.
Purton, Rowland. *Festivals and Celebrations.* Blackwell, 1979.
Shuel, Brian. *The National Trust Guide to Traditional Customs of Britain.* Webb & Bower, 1985.
Storr, Catherine. *Feasts and Festivals.* Patrick Hardy, 1983.

Visual materials

Burial, Resurrection and Ascension. Filmstrip depicting the life of Christ through Western art; part of the Life of Christ series. Available from VP Audio-visual Resources, The Green, Northleach, Cheltenham GL54 3EY.

Christian Festivals (including Whitsun/Pentecost) and *Initiation Rites* (Christian, Jewish, Sikh and Buddhist). Colour posters available from Pictorial Charts Education Trust, 27 Kirchen Road, London W13 0UD.

Christian Initiation: Infant Baptism and Confirmation (Anglican) and *Dedication and Believers' Baptism* (Baptist); *Christian Symbols.* Slidefolios in the People At Worship series. Available from Rickitt Educational Media, Ilton, Ilminster, Somerset TA19 9HS.